The Angel Inside

Michelangelo, Il Gigante, and Creating a Life of Power and Beauty

By Chris Widener

The Angel Inside

Published by
YourSuccessStore.com
2835 Exchange Boulevard
Suite 200
Southlake, TX 76092

ISBN: 0-9726266-1-1

Retail Price: $12.95

Printed in the United States of America

Foreword

I first heard Chris Widener's name in 1999. An article he had written came across my email – I read scores of personal development ezines – and this new author impressed me. Over the course of the next few years I would read every Chris Widener article that came my way. He definitely had me intrigued by his style and message.

There was something about Chris' writing that reminded me of Jim Rohn. Not the same style but the same simple, to-the-point, profound communication of timeless truths that help people lead successful lives. Week after week his articles came out on a variety of personal development and success topics. I came to believe that Chris was certainly one of the most prolific writers in the marketplace!

Because of Chris' ability to wield an unceasing pen, I contacted him in 2002 about helping Jim Rohn International develop our upcoming Jim Rohn One-Year Success Plan. After meeting Chris, we agreed that he would become our Featured Contributing Editor as well as host our monthly conference calls that would feature Jim Rohn, Zig Ziglar, Brian Tracy and other legends. With Chris' great writing skill and his talent for engaging conversation on the conference calls, The Jim Rohn One-Year Success Plan has become one of the most successful products we have ever created.

I knew that we were on to something… or rather, someone. I truly believe, as Jim does, that Chris Widener is the leader of a new generation of personal development experts.

When Chris first printed *The Angel Inside*, he sent copies to all of the staff at JRI as gifts. What happened next amazed me. We receive hundreds of books for review at our office, but this little booked burned like wildfire through our organization. People were reading and rereading it. They were reading it to their children and loaning it to their friends. Chris found that people who ordered the book would read it and then come back and order up to fifty copies to give to their friends! It is that kind of book!

Like the classic books of the great Og Mandino, *The Angel Inside* is a fable that expounds the truths of life, woven into the context of a beautiful story. *The Angel Inside* is wonderfully written and brings many descriptive words to mind: Profound, Simple, Unique, Captivating, Compelling, Refreshing and Inspiring to name a few.

The Angel Inside is a book you can – and probably will – read cover to cover. It illustrates the power that each individual has within themselves to become great and live their dreams. It will encourage you to look inward and find the person of power and beauty that is waiting to be set free to make a difference in the world.

I am convinced that you will be as impressed as my staff and I were. That is why JRI is publishing this special edition of *The Angel Inside*. We want it to be a book that will affect your life in a powerful way – and we believe that it will!

So find a quiet place and delve into this enlightening story of a young man whose life is changed forever when he meets a man – his new mentor – on the streets of Florence, Italy. Let your heart soar as you learn the lessons that were true 500 years ago, and are just as true today as they were then.

We know that you will be glad you've met Chris Widener and that you'll be impacted by the story he tells through this powerful book, *The Angel Inside*.

Enjoy!

Kyle Wilson
President
Jim Rohn International and YourSuccessStore.com

Discover the life changing principles of:
The Angel Inside

Contents

1

Finding the Angel Inside of You

"Every person has this tremendous capacity to be both king and warrior, a person of value and a person of accomplishment – of beauty and power."

Tom Cook had come to Europe looking for direction, but he was reluctantly coming to the conclusion that it may have evaded his grasp. Feeling frustrated, he had planned a two-week "getaway vacation" that he hoped would clear his head and give him the opportunity to do some soul searching. Ultimately, he was hoping that his time away from the U.S. would relieve the pressure he felt at home and allow him to make some thoughtful decisions about his future. He had already been to England, France, and Spain, but had yet to come to any clarity about himself. He was still as confused as the day he flew out of J.F.K. Today he found himself in Florence, Italy, the last city on his itinerary—and his time there was almost gone. But then, something happened….

Florence. Firenze: romance, art, food, and wine. Most who go there live an emotional high as they take in the almost overwhelming beauty of the scenery. The class of the world is held in its museums. Some of the most famous, creative, and influential names in history were born here and made their lives here. It is, in all of its glory, a cultural hub of history and art beyond comparison. One would imagine it would be the perfect place to find direction, joy, and inspiration.

About 12:45 in the afternoon, Tom was sitting on a bench in a bustling plaza. He was tired. Tired of traveling. Tired of walking. Tired of life. Tired of striving. Just tired.

As he sat with his heavy backpack on the ground below him, Tom watched a vast sea of people coming and going, running around just as he does back home. Some of the people seemed happy, others looked like they were in a frenzy to be somewhere, while still others walked along with their love, gazing at each other. But all Tom saw was a sea of people that brought more questions than answers. *Where are they going? What do they look forward to? Are they really happy?* He hated to admit it, but he was a cynic at thirty. He certainly wasn't happy and couldn't imagine that anyone else could be either. Life didn't work that way, it seemed.

As he sat, his head slowly drifted downward into his hands as he lost eye contact with the crowd around him. He was among many but was somehow still alone. Then, just as he was about to launch into a mental pity party, a voice spoke.

"My, my. You look much too young and handsome to be so sad of heart," the voice said.

Tom looked up—barely—to see the one who had interrupted his self-loathing. It was an old man. Out of courtesy, he slowly leaned back up, still not saying anything. His eyes locked on the old man, surveying his new acquaintance. The old man was somewhat of a contrast. On one hand he looked…rough. On the other hand, he had an elegant air. He was old, that was for sure. Seventy maybe? Seventy-five? He had dark brown hair and a beard that covered a craggy face. The old man was ready for a trip to the barber. Medium height, thin, but with large biceps and pillar-like forearms. They seemed out of place on the old man's body. He had a "blue collar" look about him.

But the old man's clothes revealed the taste of a connoisseur; you could tell he wasn't buying off the rack at the corner store. This was a man who knew a tailor or two. An expensive beret topped his head, and his brown hair peeked out from underneath with a flare. He wore a beautifully pattern silk shirt flowing down around the top of natty slacks. Of course, this was Italy so his leather shoes were impeccable.

The old man spoke again. "Yes, you are sad. I can tell." He didn't ask permission before he sat down next to Tom. Tom couldn't believe this was happening. He was just getting used to being alone and depressed. "But I can also see that you certainly have much to be happy about. Tell me, what is your name?"

"Tom."

"Tom? Tom… Thomas?"

"Yes, Thomas."

"Ah yes, I see. Like the doubter?" the old man grinned.

"You are doubting aren't you? Doubting Thomas. What are you doubting, Thomas?"

Tom thought to himself. *What am I doubting? This is crazy. I have a crazy Italian sitting next to me.* Finally he said, "Well, I appreciate your concern, but I am not really doubting anything."

"Pardon me, Thomas. I know you must find this intrusive, but I have intuition for these kinds of things. I have been around now forever, it seems. Yes, a very long time. I have seen much. I see that you are doubting. But perhaps you do not like that word. Well, then, what is it that burdens you this day, Thomas?"

What could it hurt? Nothing could get worse than it was. "Well, let's see. I just turned thirty years old. I'm broke. I am nowhere near where I want to be in my career. My girlfriend just dumped me because I don't have any 'upside' as she calls it. My boss thinks I have zero career potential. Even my *parents* wonder when I am going to begin to make something of myself. Frankly, I am beginning to believe I'm useless."

A young couple walked by and asked the old man if he would take their picture. He obliged, and they quickly posed for him with touristy grins. When he was finished he returned their camera and they bounded down the street, laughing giddily.

The old man turned back to Thomas "Useless, I see," said the old man. "That does sound disheartening. I can see why you would be sad, even in this beautiful city. Most people here—especially the tourists—are happy." He paused and then asked, "How long have you been in Florence?"

"This is my third day."

"Three days. That is wonderful! When do you depart?"

"Tomorrow morning at 6:30."

"Oh. Not much time left then."

The old man asked, "Have you taken in any of the artworks of interest?"

"Yes," Tom replied. "I breezed through them. What would a trip to Florence be without seeing the art, right?"

"You make a very good point, young Thomas. I myself think that the art is the most important reason to come to Florence. I assume, then, that you saw Michelangelo's work, the David—Il Gigante as they call it—The Giant?"

"Yeah, sure. That's one of the biggies, right – no pun intended?"

"Yes it is. The biggest in my opinion. And tell me Thomas, what did you learn from the David?"

"Learn? Uh, I didn't *learn* anything. I saw it. He was huge. Naked. It was great. I left."

"Oh my, you didn't learn anything from Il Gigante?" The old man looked at his watch. "It is one o'clock. Come now, we haven't much time." The old man began to stand as he said this.

Thomas looked up. "Come where? For what?" He was perfectly happy sitting right where he was. Now the old, wanna-be sage wanted to drag him off on an unscheduled tour.

"To go see Il Gigante of course! There is so much to learn from him and from Michelangelo. Come, you will see."

Okay, this is crazy. But the old man had an endearing quality. He was harmless. What else would he do for the rest of the afternoon other than watch birds land on the heads of statues?

Tom stood up and grabbed his backpack as he did. "Okay. I'm game. Let's go."

The old man beamed broadly. "Fantastic, Thomas." He put one arm around Tom and then said something that sank deeply into Tom. *"This day will forever change your life."*

With this, they began their journey to the foot of Il Gigante in the Galleria dell'Accademia. They made their way through the city walking at a pace Tom would describe as *fast. This old guy can really move!* "Excuse me, can we slow down a bit? This backpack is kind of heavy."

The old man barely turned back as he said, "Of course, pardon me. I am just excited to have you see Il Gigante again." Yet his pace slowed down very little....

Down the street, across a bridge, a right turn and then a left. Tom hadn't thought it was so far. The old man took him through an open market where he paused just long enough to buy some bread from a merchant he obviously knew. He broke it in half and handed a piece to Tom. "Enjoy!" he said as he headed off again. Tom wished he could stay and bask in the aroma of the baked goods. That had been his favorite part of Florence—the aroma of the wine, the cheese, the bread, and the fruit. *I should have eaten a bigger lunch.* Every now and then the old man would say hello to someone or pat someone on the back as they went by. *A friendly fellow.*

Finally, they arrived at the Galleria dell'Accademia. Tom had been here a few days ago. As he had mentioned to the old man, he had come because that's what tourists do when they come to Florence—they look in awe at The David. Somehow it hadn't struck him as awesome when he had come before. This time was different though. It seemed a little *other worldly.* It was a strange feeling. This time he noticed the soaring ceiling, the beauty of the room, and the sound of the hollowness of the space. People didn't speak much in the presence of the David.

Along the walls were some benches. The old man took Tom by the arm and guided him to an empty one. "Here now. Let us sit on this bench." The old man motioned for Tom to sit down almost directly in front of David. They both sat down, the old man to the right of Tom.

They just looked at it for a moment, then the old man said with a sense of wonder, "Isn't it beautiful? Just grand!"

"It's *big*, that's for sure."

"Yes! It is the Giant: Thirteen-and-a-half feet tall. It took Michelangelo twenty-eight months to sculpt him from beginning to end!"

They sat silently. Tom thought that the old man sure seemed to be enjoying himself. He was looking at the statue like a proud father. It seemed kind of weird to Tom.

Tom thought to himself, "*Well, we're in the classroom. I wonder when class begins*"?

After what seemed like an eternity, the old man said, "Thomas, do you wonder why I brought you here?"

"Sure. The thought crossed my mind. I mean, David is great and all, and I know Michelangelo was one of the greatest artists of all time, but what does that have to do with me?"

"Very good question Thomas. I have an answer. But first another question: What do you know about Michelangelo?"

"Let's see. He was Italian."

The old man laughed. "Yes, that he was."

"Other than that, he lived in the late 1400's and early 1500's."

"Yes. He died in 1564. It is more accurate to say the mid-1500's. What else?"

"He was an incredible artist who painted and sculpted."

"That's correct. Do you know what he painted and sculpted?"

"All I know is the David and the Sistine Chapel. Right?"

"Yes, those two as well as many others. Is there anything else you know about Michelangelo and Il Gigante?"

"Nope. That about covers it."

"I see." He paused to think. "Then we are ready to begin."

"All right." Tom could hardly imagine how this was going to go.

"Let us start with a story: One day, Michelangelo was working on this marble that would become David, and a young child came by where he was working. The young boy asked Michelangelo why he was working so hard hitting the rock. Michelangelo said to him, 'Young boy, there is an angel inside of this rock and I am setting him free.'" He let the story sink in. "Do you see the point of that story, Thomas?"

Tom looked at the David and thought. After running the possibilities through his mind he said, "I would guess that he meant that he was trying to make something beautiful out of the marble."

"You are on the right track Thomas. But there is more."

"How so?"

"Let me explain. In essence, you are correct. But there is more to it than meets the eye. Things specific to you; things that will mean something for you—for everyone really."

"I'm all ears!"

"Thomas, what do those who are closest to you think of you?"

"I think they like me." He then corrected himself. "They love me. But…." Tom drifted off and looked away.

"Yes?" The old man probed.

"They don't think much of what I have done with my life, or what I'm doing, or for that matter, what I'm capable of. They think of me as your basic loser, I guess."

"Hmmm. That must be painful, yes?"

"Yes." It was quite painful, in fact. Tom hadn't expected to get psychoanalyzed.

"Let me give you the history of that big piece of marble. That marble was originally cut for work before Michelangelo was even born. In fact, it was commissioned to Agostino di Duccio in 1464 – Eleven years before Michelangelo would come into this world. But eventually Agostino could not decide what to do with it, so he gave up the commission. Then, in 1476, when Michelangelo was just one year old, another artist by the name of Antonio Rossellino was commissioned to work with the marble. As with Agostino, he could not see what the marble could become. Even Leonardo da Vinci was asked to consider working the marble. He declined for two reasons: First, he thought sculpting was a low form of art. He was arrogant that way. Brilliant but arrogant." The old man rolled his eyes as if disgusted. "Second, he too could not see what that marble could become. Three artists—one of them one of the most famous ever—came before Michelangelo and could not see what that marble held deep inside. But Michelangelo, he saw the angel deep at rest within the rock, waiting to be set free to inspire Florence and the world!"

"Thomas, do you see what I am trying to teach you?"

"Sort of. Tell me more and I'll get it." Now Tom was leaning toward the statue, elbows on his knees, his chin in his hands.

"Thomas, there is an angel inside of *you*. There is a person of *beauty*. There is a person of *power*. David represented both. If you remember, the real David—the one-time King of Israel—was a very diverse fellow. Not many men have interests that broadly range from writing poetry and playing the harp to slaying giants and going to war. David, both the statue and the man, was both beautiful *and* powerful. There is a lesson there for all humans. We all have a beauty to us. We are valuable just for who we are. But we are also capable of tremendous power. We can become people of great accomplishment. We can face the giants in our lives, even as David did, and win." The old man looked at Tom to see if he was getting it. He was.

"Keep going," Tom said.

"Think of the rejection of that marble. David lay there since the beginning of time. Many people looked at it and saw *nothing*. Nothing! No potential. 'The marble was cut too thin,' many people said. But Michelangelo had the *vision* for what it could become." The old man began to turn the corner on the idea. "Do you know much about the story of the real David, Thomas?"

"Less than I know about Michelangelo." Tom grinned.

"This is okay. You will learn today – *and it will change your life forever*. There was a prophet named Samuel. God Himself told Samuel that he would find the next King in the home of a man named Jesse. So Samuel went to Jesse and told him this. Then he asked Jesse to allow him to see his sons. Jesse promptly called them together and lined them up. One by one Samuel went down the line disqualifying each son. When he got to the end he was a bit confused. He asked if there were any other sons. Jesse said there was one other, but it couldn't possibly be him. He was a shepherd, a tender of sheep. Samuel asked Jesse for his name. Jesse's answer: *David.* Jesse sent for David, and he was brought before Samuel. Samuel knew immediately that this was the next King. Jesse couldn't believe it—and his brothers didn't want to.

"To explain this to Jesse, Samuel spoke a profound truth, 'Man looks on the outside, but God, He looks on the inside.'"

"Wow!" was all Tom could say.

"Yes, this is incredible Thomas. This is the first truth that you must realize in becoming the person you desire to become. No matter what is on the outside, no matter what your life looks like now, there is an angel that lies dormant within you. Every person has this tremendous capacity to be both king and warrior, a person of value and a person of accomplishment—of beauty and power. When you understand this, when you embrace it and come to truly believe it, it will change your life forever. Your entire destiny will open before you."

"I get it in concept, but how do I believe it? I mean, there are no signs of it anywhere in my life."

"Thomas, you do not look far enough. Your eyes must search for this, deep within. Sometimes you must dwell on this truth for quite some time, every day reminding yourself of it, and then one day it becomes yours. You finally believe it. But there is a way to foster this belief. Let me ask you: What are you good at? Everyone has something that they are good at. When you know this, it is a primary indicator of what your angel will look like."

"Believe it or not, I am pretty creative. I have just never pursued it much."

"Very good then. You are a creator. This is a beautiful gift that you have. How do you use this in your work, Thomas?"

"That's the point. I don't. I got my MBA—Masters of Business Administration—and went to work for a Fortune 500 company in their mergers and acquisitions department. I crunch numbers and evaluate business plans. Then I hand it up the pipe to people who make the decisions. I'm a cog in the wheel of commerce." Tom leaned back, looked up, and sighed a sigh of desperation…or resignation.

"Tell, me, how did you end up in this business?"

"Take a guess: My dad. He is the CEO of a major corporation, makes a few million bucks a year, and flies in the corporate jet. He pushed me into it. It seems like from the third grade I was being told, 'Tom, this world isn't going to hand you anything. You have to take whatever you want. The way to get what you want is to make money. And the way to make money is in big business. Tom, here is the Golden Rule: He who has the gold makes the rules.'"

"And so you pursued money?"

"I pursued money less than I pursued business because that is what my dad wanted. I thought it would make him happy and proud of me."

"Thomas, I do not know you, yet I know many young people *like* you. You have yet to see what angel resides inside of you. The outer shell has yet to come off so that you and the world can see what beauty lies beneath. You have yet to fully display your inner value and worth. Before you can do so, you must commit to the principle and begin your search for the angel inside of you."

Tom sat silently, trying to internalize the truths the old man was speaking about. In theory he believed it, but he just couldn't see it in his own life. He had spent so many years trying to make the outside what others would like to see that he wondered if he would ever be able to find the true self that was below the surface.

After a few moments, the old man spoke. "You will not find clarity about this in one afternoon, Thomas. Yet I tell you so that the seed of this thought can be planted inside of you, and in time it will grow to become a driving force in your life. Now, you have learned the first lesson: No matter what others may say, there is an angel inside of you, waiting to be set free. In time, you will find that angel and let him soar."

"I wish my dad could hear that," Tom said.

2

The Power of Following Your Own Passion

"There comes a time in every person's life when they must decide whether they will follow what they want for their life or what someone else wants for their life."

"Thomas, this brings us to the second lesson you must learn from Il Gigante." The old man then stopped speaking, his face in deep thought.

"And that is…. What?" Tom asked.

"Yes, yes, of course Thomas." The old man had been lost in thought. "Imagine if the David had never been sculpted. Or the Sistine Chapel painted. Two of the world's greatest works of art, loved and admired by people all throughout the world." The old man was waving his hands, as he leaned closer he spoke quietly. "Now listen closely, Thomas. None of this would have been possible had Michelangelo followed his father's wishes. Nothing." He turned and looked again at the David.

"I don't get it. What do you mean nothing would have happened? What were his father's wishes?"

The old man breathed deeply. "This is very important to you, as it was for Michelangelo. Again, a story: Lodovico was the name of Michelangelo's father. He was a good man—a minor official in Florence. He owned some properties and had some money but he was losing the properties. His hope was that his children would restore the family name to its glory. He wanted his children to earn money, own properties, and befriend the ruling class. For Michelangelo, he wanted him to own a business or two, to become a merchant who would be respected in Florence. But, just like you Thomas, young Michelangelo had other ideas."

"How old was Michelangelo when this happened?"

"It started as a young boy. At thirteen he began as an apprentice for Domenico Ghirlandaio, a well-known painter. This infuriated Lodovico. This was not at all what he wanted for his boy. They argued much of the time. Lodovico did what he could to stop Michelangelo. He thought that being an artist was of the lower class."

"So what happened? I mean, I know the end of the story, but what happened that made Michelangelo do it anyway?"

The old man turned to Tom and lifted his left hand in the air, raising his index finger to make a point. "This, Thomas, is the second lesson *and it will change your life forever.*"

He certainly has a flair for the dramatic, Tom thought.

"Listen closely: No matter what others think you should do or become, *you must always follow your passion, and your passion only.* This is what Michelangelo did. He turned away from his father. He became an apprentice of Ghirlandaio and began to learn the art. Soon after, when even Ghirlandaio knew that Michelangelo was something special, Michelangelo moved into the home of Lorenzo di Medici of *the* Medici's—the most powerful people in all of Florence. Lorenzo was a patron of the arts and he put his hand upon young Michelangelo. This was very fortunate for Michelangelo!"
"What did Loda... Lovi..."

"Lodovico."

"Michelangelo's dad. What did he do?"

"There was nothing he could do. Michelangelo was pursuing his passion. It wasn't until after Michelangelo made his mark that Lodovico reluctantly gave his approval. Think for a moment, Thomas. What would happen if you simply quit what you are doing and began to do something that you love, something that burns in your heart—your *passion*?"

"My dad would kill me," Tom deadpanned.

"No, of course he would not. What would really be the problem, Thomas? Think. The answer is right there."

"He would think poorly of me." Tom looked down as he said it.

"From what you tell me, this is most likely true. He would think poorly of you. And this is exactly why your angel is still lying inside of the rock instead of standing as the warrior king. This is why you are frustrated; this is why your heart aches."

"So what do I do? I'm thirty years old, and my father has spent hundreds of thousands of dollars on my education to make me a businessman. With all due respect, I'm not a thirteen year old prodigy in 15th century Italy."

"And with all due respect, young Thomas, you are not much of a businessman either, are you?" Ouch. That one hurt, but it was just a flesh wound. "You are not a good businessman only because it is not in your heart to be a businessman. There is no passion there."

"Okay, but again – What do I *do*? Theory only goes so far."

"You quit."

"Quit my job? That's impossible."

"It is not possible, or it would not be enjoyable? There is a big difference between the two and you must learn the difference."
"Go on."

"Thomas, the world is filled with people who do not do what they love. Most people drift through life like a feather in the wind. They do not have a purpose that comes from their passion, from their strength. These are the men and women who, as it is said, 'live lives of quiet desperation.' Time passes and when they are near death, all they are left with is regret. Yet there is nothing they can do about it. Their lives are lost because they did not decide to do what they wanted. Thomas, the worst thing that can happen to you is that your father may be disappointed in you, correct?"

"Yeah, I think that's as far as it would go. I don't think he would disown me or anything like that."

"My question for you: Do you think your father is disappointed in you now?"

A long silence followed, then Tom admitted, "Yes. I'm sure he is." He hated to say it. His whole life had been devoted to pleasing his father. This larger-than-life man, so successful in everything he did, towered over his life. His father had been a 4.0 student, the quarterback on the football team, went to Harvard on a full academic scholarship, then Harvard Business School, then on to conquering the world of business. Tom had tried, but he had failed to live up to what his father wanted him to be. Part of him wanted to weep aloud right there. Another part felt free. He was beginning to be honest with himself.

"Yes, I'm sure he is, Thomas. He most likely is. Because you will never be successful doing what you do not want to do. You will certainly sabotage yourself. And this is what you need to know: Your father may always be disappointed in you, and there is nothing you can do about that, *but if you do not follow your passion, you will always be unhappy.* But there is another way: You can make the hard decision to quit and begin to follow your passion. Yes, your father may be disappointed in you, but at least you will find joy in what you do."

"I guess I really can't control what my father will think, can I?"

"Indeed. Your father is just a man, Thomas. He was once a little boy and was shaped by his parents. They poured themselves into him and he did the same to you. Humans are by no means perfect, are they? If we do not watch ourselves, we pass along many hurtful things to our children. Your father believes that money is the standard for achievement. This is not true, and you know this."

They both sat for a few minutes before the old man began again. "Thomas, there comes a time in every person's life when they must decide whether they will follow what they want for their life, or what someone else wants for their life. There will be many voices that seek to influence you. Parents will pressure you, most of the time out of good intentions because they love you. Brothers and sisters will judge your decisions and look down on you. Friends will think less of you, and some may even leave you. But there is one truth that remains: *it is your life, not theirs*. What do you think of that?"

"I think I have been living my father's life, not mine."

"It sounds like you have. But it is not too late. You are only thirty years old. Even if you were sixty, it is never too late to change and live for your passion." The old man let those words sink in and then continued, "Do you know what I find to be the most beautiful irony in this story of Michelangelo, Thomas?"

"What's that?"

"Lodovico was concerned most with money, image and class, as it appears that your father is as well, and he didn't want his son to do anything that would be considered to be of the lower class. Yet, in following his own passion, Michelangelo has set the standard and the very definition of class for *centuries*. His works of art are priceless. People travel from all over the world to see his work and gaze in wonder and awe at their exquisitely detailed beauty. Following his own passion, he was able to achieve what his father actually wanted: respect for the family name. Had he become a Florentine merchant, the world never would have known the name of Michelangelo."

Tom was thinking. His mind was racing. He felt alive, or at least like he was coming alive. The possibility of doing something besides mergers and acquisitions thrilled him. It had never been an option before, and now it was as though it could actually become a reality. The old man's words streamed through his mind.

"This day will forever change your life." He was beginning to believe that maybe, just maybe, the old man was right. He was wondering if a chance meeting on a park bench in a

country halfway across the world was fast becoming the turning point of his life. He looked at his watch. Three o'clock. They had been sitting there for close to two hours. It had seemed like minutes, and now he wanted to learn everything he could from the old man in what time remained.

"Okay," Tom said. "I got lessons one and two. What's next?"

"You are a fine student, Thomas. You learn quickly. The test will be if you remember these truths and implement them."

"I will, don't worry. What's next?"

3

Being Confident in Your Strength

"If you are to be successful, you must find self-confidence in the things that you do well, and then pursue them."

"It is time to take a closer look at Il Gigante," the old man said as he stood up and began moving toward the statue. "I will teach you a few more things here, and then I have somewhere else to take you."

Tom got up and followed until they were standing directly in front of the David. He was amazed at the size. He hadn't gotten so close the first time he came to see it. Instead, he had casually peeked his head in and then left.

"So what is the next lesson?" Tom asked.

"What do you see before you, Thomas?"

"I see… a statue."

"You are perceptive," the old man teased. "Let me be more direct: What is the mood of David?"

"The mood?"

"Yes, what do you see?"

Tom thought. "Can you give me some hints?" he asked.

"Very well. When in the battle with Goliath is the sculpture taken from?"

"I don't know."

"Before or after?" the old man prompted.

Tom looked the David over closely. Sling over the shoulder. Rock in his hand. Looking at something—Goliath—to the left. His brow furrowed in concentration. It became obvious. "Before. Right before."
"Yes, Thomas."

"Okay, why is that important?"

"A little more history for you, Thomas. Traditionally, statues of David were done so as to reflect him immediately *after* the battle. This was usually done by sculpting Goliath's head, severed from his body, at the feet of David. Michelangelo purposefully brought David to life just *before* he slew the giant. He did this because of the political situation at the time. Italy was not united. It was many fiefdoms and cities, like Florence, which constantly had to worry about attacking armies, large and small. Statues in that day were made for their beauty of course, but they were also made for powerful political statements. The statue of David was to be placed in a prominent place, the *Palazzo Vecchio*, to make a statement to the people of Florence and to anyone who would think of attacking. This is why I asked you what mood David was made to portray. Given this new understanding, what do you think David was meant to portray?"

Tom stared intently at David. He couldn't get it. "I just don't know."

"Here are the words David spoke to Goliath just before he took the sling to him, 'I will strike you down and remove your head from you. And I will give the dead bodies of the army of the Philistines this day to the birds of the sky and the wild beasts of the earth.' Now, given that these are the words David spoke to this massive giant just moments from the time where he stands here before us, what would you say David was feeling?"

Tom looked at that brow of David's. Then he thought he had it. "Confidence. He felt confident." He was sure he was right.

"Thomas, you are learning. That is exactly right. Michelangelo wanted to portray confidence. The same confidence that David showed before his battle was the same confidence that Florence was showing to those who thought of overthrowing it. Florence was saying, 'If you attack, you will die.'"

"So the lesson is *confidence*?" Tom asked.

"The lesson is that in order to achieve what you want out of life, you must be confident. And as it relates to following your passions and utilizing your strengths, you must *demonstrate* self-confidence."

"Uh, what if you don't have self-confidence?"

"Tell me Thomas, do you know what confidence means, literally?"

"No, what?"

"In the Latin it literally means 'with faith.' So you see, self-confidence means you have faith in yourself."

"But what if you don't have faith in yourself?" Tom asked.

"You must have faith in some aspect of yourself. For instance, there are many things that I do not do well. However, there are many things that I excel at. It is in these that I put my confidence. The lesson is this: If you are to be successful, you must find self-confidence in the things that you do well and then pursue them. As the David has done over the city of Florence for so many hundreds of years, *the secret is that you too must stand confidently in whatever you do.*"

"How do I do that?"

"When you go home, you begin to work in an area of your strength and talent. By doing so, you will feel and become more confident. The reason you have no confidence now is because you are not good at what you do. So you are reminded, both consciously and subconsciously, everyday, that you are not good at what you spend most of your day doing. This breeds doubt, fear, and ultimately, despair. One must work in his or her strength. Confidence comes from this."

"Check. I got it."

"Good, then we may move on?"

"I would hope so," Tom said eagerly. He was now actually enjoying being the student in the old man's classroom of life.

4

Beauty Through Details

"The masters, the ones who succeeded tremendously and set the standard for others, are those who master the details."

"Very well then, notice something else about David. I want you to walk around the statue as many times as necessary to give thought to this: Michelangelo's David is perhaps the most famous statue in the history of the world, certainly the most famous David. Tell me then, with so many David's, why is it that this statue before you has come to be known as the most beautiful? What gives *this* David its beauty? Now just walk, look, and let the answer come to you. When it does come to you, you will have learned the fourth lesson of a powerful and beautiful life." Tom was hesitant. "Go," the old man implored.

Tom began to walk, and study the David. He took nearly ten minutes, studying the David from every angle. He would walk and then stop and look for a few minutes, then continue. Finally he came back to stand next to the old man. Just as he stopped, a security guard came up to the two of them.

The guard obviously knew the old man. "Another new student today?" he asked the old man.

"Yes, and a very fine one at that."

The guard leaned close to Tom. "Pay attention. You may not know it now, but this old man has helped more people than you could ever imagine. I have seen him take people, one at a time, through here for decades. I'm sure he has told you, '*today your life will change forever.*' It's true, as you will see."

Then the guard turned to the old man again. "Keep up the good work. Set him straight." Then he was off to do more rounds.

"Good-bye" the old man said as the guard left.

Then he turned his attention back to the task at hand. "Well, Thomas, to what conclusion have you come after looking Il Gigante over so closely?"

Tom was staring at the David, "I just don't see it. I'm sorry. I'm missing something." He turned to the old man. "What is it?"

The old man smiled. "I will not give you the answer so easily, Thomas. Let me ask you this: How realistic do you consider Il Gigante?"

"Well, very realistic. It looks just like a person. Is that it?"

"That is the first part. There are many statues that look real from a distance, but when you get close you begin to see that the form is just made of marble. It ceases to be very realistic. Now look again, as closely as you can. Look at the statue to see just how closely it resembles the human form in its exactness. Go ahead," he said, as he gestured for Tom to circle the statue again. Tom took one more trip around the David.

When he had rounded David once again, the old man asked, "What is your conclusion now, Thomas?"

"It is very real."

"Yes? In what ways? Tell me what you see."

"The toes. The muscles in his legs. The tendons. The veins. His stomach and ribcage. His shoulders and arms look just like a man's. His jaw, his eyes, and his brow. And his hair. They all look real."

"Yes Thomas. This is what set Michelangelo apart from all others. These are the *details*."

"The lesson is details?" Thomas asked.

"Not quite. The lesson is that *the beauty is in the details*."

"Okay... Go on," Tom said.

"All throughout life there are people who do work of various sorts. Most people do average work. After all, that is why they call it average! Many people do above average work. The masters, the ones who succeed tremendously and set the standard for others, are those who master the details. The thing that makes an otherwise typical statue something that men and women today know in every culture is the emphasis on the details. Il Gigante finds its *beauty in the details*."

"How exactly does this apply to me?" Tom asked.

"This applies to everyone, Thomas. No matter what work you do, you must put your hand to it with the goal of absolute excellence—and excellence comes from painstaking attention to the details. In Michelangelo's day, artists were given special opportunities to dissect human cadavers so they could learn to understand anatomy. It has been jokingly said that as magnificent as Michelangelo was, he must have crucified someone so as to know firsthand the details of what Christ on the cross would truly look like. While this obviously isn't true, it *is* true that he did indeed spend time mastering the human form through dissection. He would work for hours to see how the body came together and to see how the many parts layered over one another. Then, when he would take the chisel to the marble, he would simply uncover what he had seen in the actual human body."

"Hmmm. Okay, so what about me?"

"The lesson, Thomas, is that when we are working in areas that we have no passion for, it is natural for us, with no care for our work, to simply put in the time, to do whatever will get us by and produce work that is mediocre at best and with no pleasure attached to it. Michelangelo was passionate about his work. He wanted every statue and painting to look as though it might suddenly spring to life—with a few exceptions that you will learn in a moment. Tell me Thomas, is this true for you? Do you ignore the details of your work?"

"Well, I am working with numbers and financials so I have to be somewhat exact, but I confess that most of the time I don't do the work that I could do. So no, I do not have the 'beauty of the details' as you put it."

"You see that this is all a progression, yes? Do you see that once you have the passion and the work you are good at, then you narrow down and are able to create your own lasting masterpiece of a life that is beautiful and powerful? When you get home and begin to work at what you love, not only will you have the passion to master the details, you will for the first time in your life *be able to*. This will open new worlds to you. Worlds you have never experienced before."

As Tom stared at the David, he recounted: "Everyone has an angel inside. Follow your passion. Develop your self-confidence. And finally—for now—the beauty is in the details."

"You are an excellent student. One of the best I have ever had."

Thomas remembered the words of the guard. There had been many "students" before him. He wondered who this old man was and how he could spend his days roaming the city helping wayward souls.

"Are you ready for the next lesson, Thomas?" The question jolted Tom back to the moment.

"Yes, of course. Let's go."

5

Your Hand Creates What Your Mind Conceives

"Our worlds are created through the synchronization of the creative brilliance of the mind and the diligent steadiness and skill of the hand."

"Not quite yet. There is one last lesson here before we leave. Do you remember what I said we would get to in a moment?"

"Oh yeah, you said that sometimes Michelangelo would make a part of the body not look exactly like it should, right?"

"Correct. Now, look closely again at Il Gigante. What two parts of the body are out of proportion?"

"Well, the head, obviously."

"Yes. And what else?"

Tom looked up and down the statue. He saw it. "The hands! The head and the hands." Then he repeated it for emphasis, and because he was excited that he saw it. "The head and the hands."

"That is it, Thomas. Now the important question: Why?"

"*That* I have no idea of. Why?"

"I will tell you. First, there was a practical reason why the head was so large. Michelangelo knew that the head of Il Gigante would be some twenty feet off the ground. Of course, the further away an object is, the smaller it appears. He made the head large to provide context, so it could be seen in proper proportion to the rest of the body as people looked up from the foot of the statue. There is a lesson here, but not the most important one. It is that sometimes parts of your life must be bigger than others in order to bring balance. Many people believe that we should keep everything equal, but not if you want to excel. But there is an even more important lesson that Michelangelo taught us in sculpting the head and the hands larger than they should be."

"What's that?" Tom asked.
"Did you know that Michelangelo was a writer as well, Thomas?"

"No, but it doesn't surprise me."

"Indeed, he was very good. One thing Michelangelo wrote tells of his philosophy and gives us insight into why he made the hands and the head of Il Gigante larger than they should be. In one of his sonnets, he wrote,

> "The marble not yet carved can hold the form
> Of every thought the greatest artist has,
> And no conception ever comes to pass
> Unless the hand obeys the intellect"

"Do you understand this lesson?"

"I guess that the head and the hands are both important. They have to work together?"

"In its basic premise, that is correct. Michelangelo knew that our worlds—and a statue—are created through the synchronization of the creative brilliance of the mind and the diligent steadiness and skill of the hand. It is the bringing together of the power of the mind and the delicacy of the work of the hand. This is the fifth lesson, and the final one here. *You conceive your world in your mind and then create it with your hands.*"

The old man looked at his watch. "We must be going soon, so let me finish: Thomas, you can become anything you want in life. You can achieve whatever you desire. But you must make the connection between both the head *and* the hands. Do you know what I mean?"

"Uh, not really."

"Thomas, most people live in one or the other. They either conceive of amazing things—they *dream*—but it never goes beyond that. They live only in their minds. Still others do just the opposite. They are filled with action, but not action that is thought out well. It is movement that takes them nowhere. The secret is this: *Let your mind conceive it and then let your hand create it*. True accomplishment requires both.

The old man pointed at the statue before them and continued, "As David stands facing his Goliath, he conceives in his mind what he wants to do. He sees the giant dead at his feet and his own army saved. But had he not trained by himself, slinging countless stones at trees and animals for years in obscurity, had he not been skilled enough to be able to make his hand obey his mind, the story would have ended much differently. Instead, he searches the ground and picks up five smooth stones, yet he only needs one to slay the giant. This is because his hand was trained to accomplish what his mind had decided should take place. With one demonstration of skill he launched a stone and set in motion his ascension to the throne. When the mind conceives something and the skilled hand makes it happen, you are well on your way to a powerful life. Thomas, this is the last lesson for you here. Take a good long look at David. He has been good to you today."

"Yes he has."

"Come now, let's go. We must visit a friend of mine before we eat."

"We're eating?"

"Yes, of course. You eat, don't you? We shall see my friend and teach you a few more lessons about sculpture and life. *Then,* we eat."

They started to walk out. "Okay, here we go," said Tom.

6

The Importance of Planning and Preparation

"The lesson is to not move too fast. Fast enough to get where you want to be, but slow enough to do it right the first time."

Quickly they were out on the streets of Florence again. And once again the old man was starting to outpace Tom. This time, Tom decided to let pride get the best of him and said nothing, deciding instead to just hustle along, doing the best he could to keep up with the old man. Even carrying the heavy backpack—and sweating profusely after just a few minutes—he still kept up. *This guy must have been on the Italian track team.*

In and out of the crowd they weaved. Tom did his best to keep his eye on the old man in the busy streets, all the while trying not to knock over any old women who may have ventured into his path. Suddenly the old man stopped as abruptly as he had started. He turned, waved his hand at the door to a storefront workshop in the middle of the street, and announced, "Here we are, Thomas. Your next classroom."

The old man opened the door for Tom, a bell rang and announced their arrival, though not one person looked up from his work. After you," he said, and Tom walked in, his eyes quickly scanning the room.

Interesting place, he thought.

There were about seven people in the workshop, all of whom seemed lost in their work, and each, it seemed, working on a sculpture at a different stage of completion than the others. Even with the two visitors standing in the middle of their workshop, not one person looked up from their work.

"Arturo!" the old man called out in sing-song familiarity. "Arturo! Your old friend is here!"

Almost immediately a man came out from a door in the back of the workshop. He was about fifty, short, stocky, and with the same large arms that the old man had. "Yes, it is you! I could tell from your voice. It has been what, three weeks since I last saw you?" The men embraced while Tom watched. "What brings you here today?" He looked at Tom. "Another student?"

Tom was beginning to wonder if the old man was running an unofficial school for tourists. Everybody seemed to know he did this, and on a regular basis.

"Yes, another student you may say. And this one is particularly bright. I have brought him to see firsthand how one creates a masterpiece."

"Well, you may not see a masterpiece today," Arturo said, "but you can see how one goes about creating something from the cold, hard marble."

Tom continued to look around and was actually looking forward to this. It struck a chord with his creative side.

"Please do not mind the dust. It is what comes with the trade," Arturo said.

"Another reason Leonardo didn't approve of sculpture," the old man interjected. "He didn't like to get dirty."

"Yes, well, you and I know the beauty of hard work, do we not?" Arturo asked the old man with a knowing look.

"Indeed we do."

Arturo welcomed them to walk around at their leisure. "As always, my workshop is yours. Please call me if I can help in any way."

"We certainly will," the old man replied. And with that Arturo went back to his work.

The old man looked around and took a deep breath. The workshop felt cool to Tom. There was definitely a distinct smell to it, a combination of the elements and the sweat of many hardworking sculptors, most of whom he supposed could use a shower. There was dust everywhere and the incessant sound of chisel on marble, banging, and scraping. Each of the artists worked with a sense of focus, as though they were themselves searching for their own angel.

The old man guided Tom over to the first table. On it was a relatively small piece of marble. It had yet to be touched with a chisel. When they got to the edge of the work station, the old man said, "Thomas, there are three lessons here for you to learn."

"Good. I can't wait."

"Very well, then. Take a look at this piece as it sits here. And look at the whole table. What do you see on the marble and on the table?"

"Well, on the marble I see lots of lines—I am assuming that is where the cuts will be made, or whatever you call them. On the table I see the chisels, drawings, and little wooden statues. Oh, and a clay statue."

"That is right. Now the importance of each: Creating a statue is much like creating a life in many ways. If you are going to become the person you want to become, then you will need to plan and prepare to become the person you want to become. Most people never plan for the kind of person they want to become, Thomas.

"Yet planning helps you do it right the first time. One who works with marble doesn't get many chances to cut. One mistake can ruin a whole piece. This is why it is imperative to spend time planning your work. You see the drawings? Do you notice what kind of utensil they are drawn in?"

"Pencil, it looks like."

"Correct. This is because in the drawings you can always erase and start over. Once you separate a piece of marble you can't go back. You need to do it right the first time. Sometimes in life you can go back, but it is better to get it right the first time because of good planning and preparation. *Always* do the sketching and drawing first.

"Then," the old man continued, "you do the small sculpture. This is the 'test run' I believe you Americans call it. Some use wood. Some use clay. Others may even use marble, though that isn't necessary. The idea, Thomas, is to make sure you have everything down before you cut."

"That makes sense," Tom followed.

"Then, and only then, you lay out what the sculpture will look like on the actual marble. Thomas, do you know how many people never plan—they just dream?" Dreaming isn't enough. It is a start, but then one must make sure that the dream is possible, or even desirable."

"Desirable?" Tom asked.

"Yes, desirable. Think of it for a moment, Thomas. Many students, maybe you included, grow up thinking some course of study and work would be interesting to them. They go to university and study. They do the intellectual work, and that is important. But then they graduate and begin the work and soon realize that they don't like it. By then, most people think in their minds, that it is too late. They are already settled in, they are making money, and so they continue to do something they do not enjoy.

"Many people never draw out what they want their lives to look like. They do not create the miniature sculpture to decide if the actual sculpture is what they will want to have as a finished statue."

"I'm missing something."

"Yes, of course. Think of the teacher who always wanted to help people and teach them, but when he gets into his career, he realizes that money means more to him than he originally thought. As a teacher he will never make much money. But now the teacher is stuck. He never gave significant thought to the fact that he would have certain desires for compensation. He then feels like he can't do anything else because of the investment in his education, or because he is too far into his career, or even because he is afraid of what others will think.

"Or for another example, a young person who wants to trade financial instruments realizes after a few years on the job that his personality cannot take the pressure involved. How much more enjoyment people would have in their lives and careers if they would have planned and not just studied, if they had taken the time to actually go and do what they thought would be fulfilling, instead of investing all of their money into learning about it."

"That's why we have internships, though, isn't it?"

"Thomas, did you do an internship?"

"Yes."

"And you enjoyed it?"

"Yeah, it was fine."

"Was it a clear look at what your work is in reality now?"

"Well, no."

"Exactly my point. Young people, and older people for that matter, do not do enough planning, preparation, and investigation about what they want their lives to become. They either just drift through life and allow circumstances to push them to and fro or they make rash, ill-conceived plans, then move too quickly, realizing too late that they have made a mistake, and a very bad one at that. And it is a mistake with their very life! Planning, Thomas, real planning, eliminates most of that."

"So what is the lesson for me? What can I do now?" Tom asked.

"Today you have learned many things, with a few more things to learn yet, and you have made some discoveries about yourself. Tomorrow you will begin your trip home. Your mind and heart will be free to pursue whatever you desire. You will want to move very fast because of the excitement you feel. This is all very well and good. I encourage you to take action. Yet the lesson is to not move *too fast*. Fast enough to get where you want to be, but slow enough to do it right the first time. Michelangelo had many deadlines that came with the commissions of his projects, and much of the time his pay was determined by the timeliness of his delivery."

"It helps to be the greatest sculptor who ever lived," Tom said.

"Indeed it does Thomas, but at the time, while he was well-known, he wasn't yet considered the greatest sculptor of all time. He was an artist who did do all of his planning and preparation before ever taking the chisel to the marble. And this is one of the reasons he became what he did. Plan, Thomas, *Plan*."

7

All Accomplishment Starts With One Swift Action

"Action is the beginning of accomplishment. Without it, you have only wasted dreams and good intentions."

As the old man finished speaking, he saw out of the corner of his eye another young man, probably an apprentice, who looked like he was about to begin on a fresh piece of marble. "Excuse me," the old man said to the artist, "but are you about to begin with that?" He motioned to a small piece of marble, about three feet long.

"Yes I am," said the artist.

"Very good. Do you mind if we watch?" He started to move over to the place where the artist was working. Tom followed.

When they reached the workbench, the young artist picked up one of the larger chisels and positioned it carefully. Then, with one swift blow, he brought the hammer down and took off a large piece of the marble.

"What will this be when you are finished with it?" the old man asked.

"I am hoping it becomes a lion," the artist said.

"It will be, and it will be beautiful," the old man said, hoping to encourage him. "It will take some detail to make it work. I hope you are good." He smiled.

"I'm pretty good," said the artist, also smiling.

"Well, continue to work. My friend and I will not bother you." With that the old man backed up a bit and took Tom with him by tugging slightly at the elbow.

"We're leaving already?" Tom asked. "That's it?"

When they were about six feet away, the old man finally replied, "Thomas, what you just saw was one of the most simple and yet profound lessons any human being could ever learn. In fact, many people live in prisons of forgone dreams because they do not learn the lesson we just saw. Do you know what it is?"

Thomas was just baffled. He couldn't think of one profound idea he just learned from watching the young apprentice take a whack at the marble, and he told the old man so. "Well, to be very honest, I can't imagine what profound lesson I just learned watching him for twenty seconds. You are going to have to tell me or I'll never get it."

"Yes, this one is so simple that many people do not see it. Yet, it is extremely important. Here it is, Thomas: *Every successful endeavor begins with one swift action.*

"That's it? That's profound?" Tom still didn't get it.

"Think for a moment Thomas. How many people have dreams deep within them?"

"Practically everyone I guess."

"Exactly. Everyone. Now, what percentage of people actually lives their dreams? Or what percentage even *pursue* their dreams?"

"Well, much fewer."

"In the grand scheme of things Thomas, virtually no one pursues their dreams. Yes, they dream. In fact, I believe that we humans are born dreamers. Some even plan, or prepare. But very few ever *start*. And therein lies the problem. Thomas, you have learned much here today, and there are a few more insights I have for you. The key to your success when you get home will be whether you apply what you have learned here or if you write it off as the rants of a crazy old man. But here is the truth: This artist could plan and prepare for weeks, but if he doesn't pick up the hammer, aim, and then strike the marble, he will never get to that beautiful lion that I am sure resides within him. He must start, that is the key. Action is the beginning of accomplishment. Without it, you have only wasted dreams and good intentions."

"So why do you think most people don't start?" Tom asked.

"I think there are a number of reasons. One is that they never give it enough thought to actually bring themselves to a place of action. Another reason is that they do not plan and lay out a strategy. Still another is that they are just enough engrossed or tied into what they are currently doing that they cannot start on their dreams. For example, a man may have a dream of becoming a writer, but he makes $100,000 a year, has a company car and a nice retirement package. His wife doesn't work and the kids are in private school and taking piano lessons. So he asks himself if he will quit and pursue his dream. The answer is almost always 'no.'"

"Yeah, that sounds like most people."

"But the last reason is perhaps the most powerful reason that people never start. That reason, Thomas, is *fear*."

"Fear? Fear of what?"

"Fear of anything. Fear of everything. For example, what are you fearful of that would keep you from leaving your work and pursuing your creative side?"

"Fear that my father would think I was stupid."

"I figured you would say that. For most, that fear paralyzes them, and they never start. Some people are afraid of failing. Others are afraid of not being able to provide for their families. Others are afraid of losing their reputation. There is the ubiquitous fear of change. Some are even afraid of *succeeding*."

"Succeeding? Why would anyone be afraid of succeeding?"

"They are afraid they won't be able to perform at that level, afraid of the responsibility that power and wealth may bring, and eventually they become afraid of falling from a much higher level. You know, a drop from one foot isn't nearly as bad as a drop from twenty."

"I guess I never thought about that before."

"Fear, Thomas, is the driving factor for many who do not take the simple step of starting. Let me ask you: What would you like to start when you get home?"

Tom looked up as he thought, and then said, "Well, it's funny you mentioned piano lessons. I have always wanted to learn to play the piano. I am amazed whenever I see someone play beautiful music."

"So why haven't you ever taken lessons before?"

Tom had a surprised look come across his face.

"Ultimately... I'm scared." He had never thought of it that way before.

"Scared of what?"

"Scared of not being talented enough to actually do it. Scared of what my dad will think. He thinks most musicians are sissies. I just have never wanted to deal with it."

"And so you have never started. You see, *fear*. But that is okay. Now you know this of yourself. When you get home you must take a swift action to start."

"Like what?"

"Open the phone book, pick up the phone, and set the appointment for your first lesson. Simple, isn't it? Yet whether or not you ever learn to play the piano depends on that simple step. You must look at your fears and then defeat them."

"Yes, I need to," Tom conceded.

"Imagine if Michelangelo had done what those other artists had done: Thought about what to do with the marble but never started. Who knows, that marble may still be sitting there today." He paused while it settled into Tom. Then he winked as he said, "And I would have no stories to teach you these lessons with!"

"And they are good lessons," Tom said. "Are there any more?"

"Yes, a few short lessons before we leave and enjoy our meal. I *am* getting hungry, so we mustn't spend too much time here."

"Okay, what are they?"

8

Embracing the Stages of Chipping, Sculpting, Sanding and Polishing

"We must go through the same progression: Chip away what doesn't belong, sculpt our lives and give them form through the people we associate with and the information we take in, allow the rough spots of our lives to be sanded away through adversity and suffering, and then and only then, are we ready to be polished and let our power and beauty show in all of its glory."

"Here, come to the center of the room with me." They walked toward a spot where the old man could show Tom the whole room. "Look around. All of these sculptures are at different stages. They all have different work being done on them. Essentially though, there are only four acts that take you from the raw material to the finished piece. They are chipping, sculpting, sanding, and polishing. That is the bulk of the work that is to be done."

"Okay… and what is the significance of that?"

"I like to think of life that way. We must understand that there are times when the Supreme Artist chips away at us, other times when he is sculpting us, other times when he is sanding, and then times when he is polishing. All of these are needed to create a beautiful life, just as they are needed to create a beautiful sculpture."

"Okay, I can see that."

"The problem, Thomas, isn't whether people can see it, but whether they can accept it. And furthermore, most importantly, whether they can *embrace* it."

"Embrace it?"

"Yes. *Embrace it.* You see, if we simply accept it, we are still not necessarily a willing participant in the process, that is, we are not necessarily participants with good attitudes. That is key: a good attitude about the process."

"Okay, so explain the difference between them."

"Very well. Let's start with chipping, for lack of a better word. Every person has parts of them that simply must go.

If those parts stay, you might never see the Angel Inside. If we are going to create a life of power and beauty, we must allow ourselves to go through the processes that chip away at all of the peripheral parts of us that hide our true selves. Yet most people do not embrace this."

"Why?"

"Pain. People are afraid of pain. Physical pain. Emotional pain. Psychological pain. When we lose parts of ourselves, even bad parts that keep us from growing as humans, it hurts. It hurts because we have become comfortable with our negative aspects. We have learned to compensate for them. So, rather than allow them to be chipped away at, we run away from the process. And because of that, we are stuck where we are and our Angel never comes to the surface."

"Hmmm."

"Yes, give this some thought Thomas. It is important. You have parts of you that must die and fall away if you are to become the person who you want to become, who you are *destined* to become. If you do not allow the chipping away of the exterior, you will forever hide the Angel Inside."

The old man moved his head left to right, looking for another artist he could use to make his next point. When he spotted one, he pointed him out and said, "There, do you see the young man at that table wearing the blue smock?"

"Sure," Tom replied.

"He is an example of the next lesson. Do you see how he is using a different chisel than the one used to take off large portions of the marble?"

"Yes."

"He is in the process of sculpting. This is different than chipping in that chipping is where you take off what doesn't belong. But sculpting is the fine art of slowly and delicately revealing the form and beauty of the piece, the details we spoke of earlier. This is where the artist makes the piece become what it is intended to become. There is a lesson for life in this."

"I think I could guess, but tell me, how so?"

"Well, when we have allowed life and our own actions of discipline to eliminate that which hides our true inner selves, we then must actively form the life that we want to lead."

"How do you do that?"

"There are many tools for this, Thomas. The tools of a sculptor are few, but the tools for sculpting a life are many. We are a product of the things that we allow to shape and influence our lives. Everything that we interact with will shape and mold whom we become. This includes both what we choose to involve ourselves with, as well as what we choose not to involve ourselves with."

"Give me some examples," Tom requested.

"Let me start with what we choose to involve ourselves with. First and foremost are the people who we involve ourselves with. Our business associates and our friends are people who we can choose at will. We should choose these people wisely for what they will help us become. We should seek out those who will challenge and encourage us to become the very best that we can become. The goal is to have a network of people around us who act as a springboard to a better life."

"That makes sense. What is the second?"

"The second is like it; it is the books that we read."

"Books?"

"Yes, books. I like to view books as the ability to converse with the author. I like to imagine that the author is speaking these ideas to me. I react and ask questions in my mind as I read, allowing me to 'converse' with the author. This way I am not bound by the limitations of time and space. I can be friends with the greatest minds that walk, and have walked, the earth. I can have them speak into my life and challenge my thinking, all the while having them shape my life and help me become a better person, a more successful person."

"I have never thought of it that way before. All those years I hated reading in school!"

"Yes, many people view books as boring and a waste of time, yet if they view it as an opportunity to sit down with the author and learn from them, we open ourselves to whole new levels of learning and growth. The lesson here, Thomas, is that our lives are sculpted and formed primarily by the people we associate with and the books we read. When people grasp that concept, they are prepared to shape their lives into what they want them to become. You understand, yes?"

"Sure. I am going to get some good books when I get home and 'make friends' with some people who I have never met before, people who will make me better."

"Yes, but one more piece of advice on the reading of books. I want to encourage you to spend most of your time reading men and women who have passed on long ago."
"You mean dead guys?"

"Well, I wouldn't have described it that way, but yes, this is exactly what I mean."

"Why dead guys?"

"It is not because of the people themselves per se, but the fact that if their books are still touching and helping people, their ideas must be lasting, and what you are looking for are ideas that have passed the test of time. You should look for *timeless* content, not *vogue* content."

"Yeah, that makes sense. I don't read a lot of dead guys."

"Now you will," said the old man as he turned to find another artist at another table. When he saw what he was looking for, he again directed Tom's attention there: "Can you tell what that young man is doing?"

"Well, it looks like he's sanding the statue. What is it, a cherub?"

"That is what it looks like from here. And yes, he is sanding it. Do you know what sanding represents in a life, Thomas?

"When you are being worn down?" he guessed.

"That's close. In a sense it is when we are worn down. But it is much more positive than that. Sanding represents those times in our lives when *seemingly* negative circumstances surround us. It is when things grate against us. They can be irritable if we let them. People… circumstances… they all perform the act of sanding."

"So what is positive in that?"

"Again, most people seek comfort in their lives. They avoid suffering and adversity. Yet almost all people of significance and accomplishment have tremendous lessons of adversity or suffering in their past. These times of suffering and trials are what give people substance. They are what give our lives meaning. They are what keep us humble when we finally succeed. They give us appreciation. They keep us from simple answers about life, because there are none. As the Good Book says, 'trials produce perseverance, perseverance, character, and character, hope.' Wisdom indeed. Yet most people run from trials, and they never learn to persevere. They either learn to quit or hide. And there is no power in that, is there, Thomas?"

"It doesn't seem so."

"Trials, adversity and suffering, sanding if you will, are all a significant process of shaping our lives… if we handle them correctly."

"What is 'correctly'?"

"There are three main ways to make sure we handle these times correctly. One is to accept that they are a part of life and to embrace them. The second is to have a good attitude about our lives, even when they are not going well. The third is to seek to learn from the situations, about ourselves, about the world, about life, and about people. And lastly, we must the find opportunity in negative circumstances. Every negative situation can bring a positive outcome if we look for the good that can come from it. Those who are successful are those who can turn adversity into achievement. Give that some thought as well, young Thomas."

"I certainly will."

The old man had already spotted the next person he wanted to point out and directed Tom's eyes there. "Of course you can see what this young lady is doing there."

"I am assuming from the shine she's putting on that, that you are talking about polishing."

"Correct. Polishing – the final step. The one that represents the part of life that everyone wants to skip to."

"What's that?"

"This represents the part of life that make's us look good. It is when we let the world see how beautiful we are. It is when we 'shine' so to speak. It is when our Angel stands before the earth in its full glory. These are the times when we are seen by the world around us in all of our beauty and power. Everyone loves these times, don't they?"

"Well, they beat a sharp stick in the eye, that's for sure!" The old man looked at Tom quizzically. He had never heard that phrase before. Tom could tell and added, "You know, it beats the bad times."

"Yes, of course. The polishing is certainly the enjoyable part. It is what gives us our finish. But the lesson here is that the polishing must come last. Michelangelo would have created nothing had he just started with polishing that marble. First he had to chip, sculpt and sand. Doing these things brought him to where he could finish by polishing Il Gigante, thus leaving the world with his lasting work of power and beauty. The same is true with life, Thomas. We must go through the same progression: Chip away what doesn't belong, sculpt our lives and give them form through the people we associate with and the information we take in, allow the rough spots of our lives to be sanded away through adversity and suffering, and then, only then, are we ready to be polished and let our power and beauty show in all of its glory."

"So does that mean we can't accomplish much when we're young?"

"You have brought up a brilliant exception to my point. In life we do not wait until the final days of our lives to shine, though most people accomplish their most significant work later on in life and make their greatest contributions there. In life there are many times when we can shine, but the point is that it will always come after the other work has been done first."

Tom stared at a nearby block. "What are you thinking Thomas?" the old man asked.

"I am just feeling a little overwhelmed with all of the information. It is all great... it's just so much."

"I know, Thomas. Your mind will remember what it needs to, and then when you get home, remind yourself everyday so you can learn and apply them slowly as you go."

"That's a good idea."

"Yes, it is. As is the idea to get dinner! Are you ready for some of Italy's finest cuisine?"

Thomas realized that he really was getting hungry. "I sure am! And I'll bet you know a good place."

"I know a haunt or two," the old man said with a smile. "Let's go." With that, they both turned to leave. As they walked out the door, the old man turned inside again. "Good-bye my friend, Arturo! I will see you soon!" Without waiting for an answer, they both walked out the door.

9

Being Content: Sometimes Success Takes Years

"Sometimes success just takes years. It takes methodical action over time."

The old man turned left as they exited and began down the sidewalk. This time, however, he was going at a much slower pace. That suited Tom just fine. The old man seemed to be preparing for a leisurely dinner as they walked to the restaurant. He was talkative and pointed out different places of interest as they went.

They had been walking about ten minutes when they arrived at the restaurant. It was a small place, with only ten or twelve tables. Some of the tables were set up al fresco, as the Italians enjoy. There was a large chalkboard just to the left of the door with a menu on it. They stopped and read it.

"Come, let's sit down. I will order for us," the old man declared. That is, if you don't mind. I am pretty good at this."

"No. Certainly. If you like it, I am sure I will too."

The old man caught the eye of the server and pointed to one of the tables on the small terrace. He gave them the okay and Tom and the old man sat down.

Soon the server brought some pane and olive oil for them to start with. "Would you like water this evening," he asked.

"Yes, by all means. One bottle. Flat."

"Very good. Any questions on the choices?"

"No, I believe we are fine."

"I will be right back then."

Tom and the old man both leaned back in their chairs and enjoyed the warmth of the setting sun.

The waiter returned. "What would you like this evening?"

"I will order for the both of us," the old man began. "We would like to start with a carafe of the house red."

"Yes sir."

"And for dinner we would like the following: Antipasti. Primi, do you have a risotto?"

"We sure do."

"Then a formaggio Gnocchi. Secondi, what would you recommend?"

"We have a very good fresh halibut with asparagus and a light wine sauce."

"That sounds delicious. We'll have that. And for Piatto Principale, I am hoping you have Lamb with Parmesan cheese and eggs."

"That we do."

"That sounds perfect. And of course your selection of fruit and cheese. And maybe, just maybe, we may indulge in dolce. But we will decide on that then."

"Thank you," said the waiter before leaving them to themselves again.

"It sounds like you ordered for an army," Tom said.

"A small army of two," replied the old man.

The server brought the carafe of wine and after he poured it, the old man held his glass for a toast. To all you have learned today. *May it change your life forever!*" They clinked glasses and took their first sip.

"Very good," Tom said.

"Yes, I like this trattoria very much."

For the next ten minutes or so, the old man peppered Tom with questions about the other legs of his trip, hearing all about the places he visited. Tom was somewhat excited because of all he was able to experience, but still in the back of his mind, he was disappointed that the other places hadn't helped him find the answers he came looking for. At least he was glad that he had found the old man, or had the old man found him? In any case, he was grateful for the lessons he was learning. They were simple, yes, but profound, and just what he needed to hear at this stage in his life.

Soon the first course of the meal was brought to the table.

Tom dug in with vigor. He hadn't realized how hungry he had been, and in order to save money on his trip, he had eaten less than the best cuisine. The smell in the restaurant had been overwhelming as he waited for his meal to arrive, so when it did, he wasted no time starting.

"How does it taste?" the old man asked after Tom had a few bites in him. "Is it up to your standards?"

"Mmmm. Absolutely." Tom was barely done with his bite as he spoke.

"You look like you haven't eaten in a week."

"If you're talking about food this good, I haven't! Two weeks actually!"

"Well, enjoy. This is my treat, you know."

"Thank you very much. I intend to take advantage of it," Tom said with a smile.

"I normally don't like to be taken advantage of, but it is acceptable this time." With that, the old man lifted his glass of wine again and held it toward Tom. Tom reciprocated and the old man said, "To your coming success," as they touched their glasses together.

"So, what is the next lesson?" Tom asked.

"You are an eager learner indeed."

"Well, time is short. Let's start."

"Very well, we should begin then."

"What's the first lesson of the dinner hour?" Tom asked.

"Thomas, before I give you the lesson, let me ask you: Where do you *think* you should be by now, as far as your career is concerned?"

"Well, I think that I should be making almost half again as much money, and at least two tiers above where I am in the organizational chart."

"Really?"

"Yes, really. Why?"

"Because that seems unreasonable."

"Why is that unreasonable? I read about people all the time who have much more success than I do at the same age."

"You have hit upon a good point I must address. Yes, the media focuses on the very successful, but have you ever asked yourself what percentage they represent of the overall population? What percentage of 30 year-olds like yourself are directors of corporations making $125,000 a year?" he paused briefly and then continued. "Thomas, it is miniscule. Of course, the media must cover them. A magazine article on a 30 year old making $20,000 a year and stuck in the middle of the pack is hardly inspiring."

"True."

"Very true. So here is the lesson: *Sometimes success takes years*. And sometimes years and years. Did you know that Il Gigante is 13 and one-half feet tall? It took Michelangelo 28 months to sculpt the statue from start to finish. That is less than 6 inches per *month* or less than one and a half inches per *week*. Michelangelo's successful completion of the David was *slow* any way you look at it. Yet he knew that the time and patience would be well worth the wait. Life is also like that. Sometimes success just takes years. It takes methodical action over time."

"But…" Tom tried to say something.

"There are no but's, Thomas! I lovingly say to you that you place too much pressure on yourself to succeed. You are telling yourself that you should be far more ahead of where you are. This just isn't true."

"But life is short. You have to get it while you can."

The server quietly interjected the next part of the meal as he would the rest of the evening. The old man waited to speak until after the server left the table.

"I agree wholeheartedly that life is short. Remember, you are talking to an old man here. I am older than you could possibly imagine, and yet I know that life must be paced. There are seasons to life. There is a season to build the home and a season to live in it. There is a season to tend to the crops and a season to bring them in and eat them. There are seasons of life, Thomas, and you are in the beginning season. You will get to that point in your life before you know it. And when you do, you will most likely long for the earlier season. The earlier we are in our lives the more we hope for the latter stages, and the later we get in life, the more we long for earlier times. The key is to enjoy each stage and understand that success takes time."

"Okay, so how do I get over the thoughts that I have about where I am?"

"That is a fair question. I will do my best to answer. Thomas, I find the human mind to be fascinating. It is an incredible work of art in and of itself. The amazing potential of the mind is that we can shape what the mind will become and believe."

"How so?"

"By what we think about. The mystery is that we think about what we tend to think about. If we think about how hard things are, then we tend to worry about how hard things are. If we focus on being grateful for our lives and what we have, our thoughts will tend to be thoughts of gratitude."

"Okay, so how does that apply to me and the fact that I am disappointed in what I have achieved?"

"Imagine: Do you think Michelangelo stopped every day after completing another portion of the David and said to himself, 'I will never get this done. I should be further along'? Or do you think that he kept in the forefront of his mind that little by little he was completing his masterpiece and soon enough it would be done?"

"That makes sense. So what should I think?"

"What do *you* think you should think?"

"That I should enjoy where I am. That I should take the time I need to learn what I will need for the next stage of my life. That I will get to that stage soon. How are those?"

"They are as good of a start as I think you can make. When you get home, begin to tell yourself these things each day. Take the time a few times each day to make those statements to yourself. In doing so, over time, you will reshape your thoughts to become the thoughts you desire."

"Check. I'll do it. What's next?"

10

No One Starts With The Sistine Chapel

"Live your life and do your work in the embodiment of excellence, and all the opportunities will flow your way. People cannot, they will not, turn an eye away from excellence."

"The next is the final lesson – a lesson similar to the one that you just learned. Here it is: *No one starts with the Sistine Chapel.*"

"Catchy title anyway."

"Thank you," the old man said with an accompanying wink. "But let me tell you what I mean by that. Many young people like yourself, and even anyone at the beginning stages of a new venture for that matter, pressure themselves to produce tremendous results as soon as they start."

"Shouldn't they?"

"Life isn't like that Thomas. In theory it would work, but in life… rarely. Let me give you the example from the life of Michelangelo. You see, Michelangelo, while being known for painting the Sistine Chapel, certainly didn't start with that. No, there were three pieces of work that he did over a period of years before this brought him, one by one, to higher and higher steps of achievement, culminating in his Sistine Chapel work. When he was seventeen Michelangelo did a low relief project in marble called the Battle of the Centaurs. This is what put Michelangelo on the map so to speak. It was a phenomenal work for anyone, let alone a seventeen year old. So he achieved something as a young man, but more was certainly to come."

"What was his next big thing?"

"His 'next big thing' was what I believe to be not only Michelangelo's most magnificent work, but the greatest sculpture ever done."

"Really, what was it?"
"It is called the Pieta. Do you know it?"
"Hmmm. It sounds vaguely familiar, but I don't know."

"Some would argue that two other statues were the next big things, and of course they were very good, but I see the Pieta as the next monumental piece in Michelangelo's history."

"What were the other two?"

"Oh yes. The first was Saint Proculus. The second was Bacchus. Both are wonderfully done, but the Pieta…." The old man closed his eyes, obviously picturing the sculpture in his mind and savoring its beauty.

"That good, huh?"

The old man opened his eyes. "Better than 'that good.' The Pieta is simply stunning. Did you go to St. Peter's in Rome?"

"No. I skipped that."

"Unfortunate. You will have to come back someday and bring someone with you. Everyone should see the Pieta."
"You have me intrigued. What is it?"

"The Pieta is breathtaking. I can barely describe it, and I know it as well as anyone. Nothing I can say would do justice to the beauty of the work. It is a sculpture of Mary, seated, with the dead Christ lying across her lap. She gazes down at her dead son. It is moving, disturbing, haunting… and yet inspiring. Yes, you must see it someday, Thomas."

"Well, now I will. I wish I could go back, by the way you describe it."

The old man quickly turned back to the original topic. "Number three. Can you guess what that was?"

"It must be the David?" Tom stated more than asked.

"Correct. And of course number four was the Sistine Chapel, the most dramatic painting ever accomplished. It is better than anything Leonardo did, I believe. There are a few important lessons to be learned from this bit of history, Thomas."

"For example?"

"*No one starts with the Sistine Chapel.* No, most people cannot accomplish the great work that will be lasting until they have gone through the process of growing and learning from their experience. Of course, there are a few exceptions, but for the vast majority of people, their life work is a process and a progress."

"What do you mean by a 'progress'?"

"I mean that young people, while they can do wonderful work—and they bring so much energy and vigor—they must go through the process of life and experience. They must become accomplished. They must meet the people who will open doors for them and help them produce their work of beauty and power. Many young people, and I think you too, are impatient in allowing their lives to unfold. You will soon learn the brevity of life, Thomas. But there is another lesson here."

"What is it?"

"Whatever you have as your work, do it with excellence. Excellence is what will open the door for further opportunity. Many young people want opportunity, but here is a secret for the ages: Live your life and do your work in the embodiment of excellence, and all the opportunities will flow your way. People cannot, they will not, turn an eye away from excellence."

"So how do I do that, I mean, practically speaking?"

"The first thing is to live in the moment. Yes, we should dream. We should have visions of what lies ahead for us. But what will take us there is not the dream of it, but the excellence we demonstrate each and every day. The excellence we have in our work will last long enough for someone in the future to see. The excellence in our relationships will pay its dividends later on in life when someone we met and were kind to will return the favor and give us an opportunity that we may have not otherwise had. The excellence we demonstrate in our character will provide us the foundation of a life well lived in every area. In the end, we will reflect back on our lives as people who are deeply satisfied not only in what we have accomplished, but even more importantly, in what we have become, for a person with accomplishments that is not coupled with an accomplished character, is not a life of accomplishment. Do you understand?"
"I think so."

"Leave it with this: Enjoy yourself now. Live your life with excellence. Become a person that others will be proud to know. Do the best you can at your work. And everything that is destined to come to pass will indeed come to pass."

"I hope so."

"It will be so, Thomas. I know these things. People can change. Believe it or not, I used to have a reputation for being somewhat of a curmudgeon, but I learned some things about people… and I changed. You have a tremendous future ahead of you as you change."

"Well thanks. You're too kind… or just gullible. Let me ask you: What did you used to do. For work, I mean?"

"What do you think?"

"I'm guessing sculpture."

"You guess right. How did you know."

"Obviously your understanding of art. But what made me sure of it was seeing Arturo's arms and noticing the

similarity to yours. That is what made me think sculpture."
The old man just smiled. "So, do you still do sculpture?"

"No, I am retired. Now I just teach my informal students
such as yourself."

"So what did you do? What did you sculpt?"

"Oh, various things, statues and reliefs. The typical. I
painted a little here and there. I was a good painter, but it
was working with marble that I loved the most."

"Just like Michelangelo."

"Yes, exactly like Michelangelo."

With the lessons out of the way, Tom and the old man
spent the balance of their time together talking about Italy,
the old man playing the part of virtual tour guide and
historian. Tom found it all fascinating.

When they were through with their delicious dinner, they
got up and walked to the sidewalk.

"Thomas, meet me in the morning before you go so I can see you off."

"Sure, I would like that. I need to leave shortly after six, so we could meet at six."

"That would be fine. There is a large plaza on the north side of your hotel. I can meet you at the fountain there. Six a.m.?"

"Sharp. I'll be there, bags ready to go."

"I will see you then."

"Thanks for dinner tonight."

"It was my pleasure, Thomas. Good evening." The old man turned and disappeared into a group of people. Tom watched for a moment, even after he couldn't see the old man any more, and then decided it was time to get to bed. Just as Tom turned to head back to his hotel, the old man tapped him on the back. He was holding a piece of paper.

"I have saved you some time. Read this when you get back to your room. And I will see you tomorrow morning." Tom took the paper and the old man turned again into the night.

After the short walk in the cool of the night, Tom arrived back in his room and opened the paper the old man had given him. On it were the lessons he had learned that day:

- ➤ Find the Angel within you
- ➤ Follow your own passion
- ➤ Be confident in your strength
- ➤ The beauty is in the details
- ➤ The hand creates what the mind conceives
- ➤ Plan and prepare
- ➤ Start with swift action
- ➤ Embrace the stages of chipping, sculpting, sanding and polishing
- ➤ Sometimes success takes years, so be content
- ➤ No one starts with the Sistine Chapel

The old man really was prepared to teach someone today. As he lay in his bed, slowly drifting to sleep, Tom finally believed that maybe today his life truly had changed forever.

It was six a.m. on the button and the old man and Tom were walking toward each other from the opposite sides of the plaza. There was virtually no one else there. A few shop owners were preparing to open for the day ahead, some even sweeping outside a few feet. Only Tom and his teacher were in the middle of the plaza. They reached one another and shook hands.

"Good morning, young Thomas."

"Good morning to you," Tom replied.

"Today your journey begins. Where it takes you is up to you."

"Yes, I know. But with what you have shown me, I think I'm ready."

"When do you leave?"

"In just a few minutes actually; I can't talk long." They stood alone in the plaza, looking at one another, the old man smiling and Tom with small tears in the corner of his eyes. He couldn't believe what had happened. An old man appeared out of nowhere and taught him the greatest lessons he had ever learned about life and happiness.

"Hey, by the way, I would like to keep in touch. Can I have your address?"

The old man looked at Tom in the face for a moment, deciding. "Thomas, perhaps you can give me your information. A business card maybe. Then I can follow up with you. Is that alright?"

"Yeah, sure," Tom replied. He pulled out his wallet and found one, slightly bent, and handed it to the old man. "There you go. All the information is right. Be sure to get hold of me."

"Well then, I guess this is goodbye," the old man said.

"Yes, it is goodbye. Thank you. Thank you for everything," Tom said.
And there the two embraced like a father and a son. "You are very welcome, young Thomas," the old man whispered in Tom's ear.

Tom pulled back and readied himself to leave. "I'll see you then."

"Goodbye."

Tom turned and began walking away while the old man simply watched. After just a few steps, Tom turned back. The old man was waiting.

"You know, I never even asked you your name. What *is* your name?"

"Thomas, you may call me *Mr. Bounarroti*."

"Okay then, Mr. Bounarroti. Goodbye." He turned to leave and started walking, but after just a few steps a thought crossed his mind, *Bounarroti. Bounarroti? That's familiar. Where have I seen that before? The plaques! That was Michelangelo's last name: Bounarroti.* He stopped in his tracks and spun back to the old man. What he saw amazed him.

He saw… *nothing.*

The old man—Michelangelo himself—was gone.

Evidently, just as there is an angel inside of each and every person, a special angel still roams the city of Florence helping others learn about art and life.

11

Angel Inside Discussion Guide and Workbook

Find the Angel Inside You

- What do you *think* about the concept of the Angel Inside?

- How do you *feel* about the concept of the Angel Inside?

- In what ways have you felt "hidden" beneath the marble?

- Have you ever felt like others just can't see the "real you"?

- In what areas of strength can you begin to live out that will reveal the Angel Within?

Follow Your Own Passion

- Would you say you are following your own passion right now? Why?

- In what ways have others tried to get you to follow their passion for your life rather than letting you follow your own?

- What would happen in your life if you began to follow your own passion?

- What would you have to do or change to be able to follow your own passion?

- Are you willing to take the risks necessary to follow your own passion?

- What are the roadblocks to following your own passion?

- What would life be like for you if you were able to live out your passion and make your dream a reality?

Be Confident in Your Strength

- What are your strengths?

- How confident are you of your abilities in general?

- How confident are you when you are operating out of your strengths?

- If you don't know what your strengths are, ask some friends to help you and then record their answers here:

- How can you imagine your life changing if you could live more fully out of your strengths in your life?

The Beauty is in the Details

- Would you say that you are a "detail person" by nature?

- If not, how would you rate your attention to detail?

- What do you think would happen if you could double your attention to detail in your life?

- How can you see your work life improving if you paid more attention to the details?

- How can you see your home life improving if you paid more attention to the details?

The Hand Creates What the Mind Conceives

- How well would you say you understand and apply the concept described here?

- Which do you have a tendency to focus on: The work of the mind or the hand?

- How much time do you spend conceptualizing? Can you establish a regular time to set aside for "dreaming"?

- What three specific actions can you take to implement the conceptions of your mind?

Planning and Preparation

- On a scale of one to ten, how would you rate yourself on planning?

- On a scale of one to ten, how would you rate yourself on preparation?

- If you don't rate yourself very high in planning and preparation, are there any areas of your life that you plan and prepare well in? If so, why do you suppose that is?

- In what ways could you take simple steps to plan and prepare better?

- Do you have a set time each day or week that you devote to planning and preparation?

- Can you think of a time when you planned and prepared and the situation turned out great? How did that feel?

Start with Swift Action

- What would you like to achieve that you simply have not acted on?

- What keeps you from action in general?

- What is keeping you from taking action today or tomorrow?

- What three action steps could you take now to begin accomplishing your dream?

Embrace the Stages of Chipping, Sculpting, Sanding and Polishing

- What is one thing that you know you must remove from your life in order to allow your Angel Inside to shine through?

- What area of your life do you already see needs some sculpting?

- Are you going through any sanding right now? If so, what are you learning? If not, can you think of how you have been made better in the past from a time of sanding?

- When was the last time you felt like you had been polished and set up for people to admire? Have you ever felt that way? If not, how would it feel to be in that place?

Sometimes Success Takes Years: Be Content

- Have you ever felt like you weren't content? In hindsight, did it do you any good?

- Can you explain how we can be both ambitious and content at the same time?

- In what ways would it benefit you to be content right now?

- In what area can you see that success will come if you are content and let your life run its course?

- How can you change your thinking to help you become more content?

No One Starts with the Sistine Chapel

- What "Sistine Chapel" would you like to accomplish one day?

- What stages have you already gone through, and must you go through, in order to achieve the things that you want to achieve?

- Do you pursue excellence at every stage in order to give yourself the opportunity to grow to the next stage?

Final Questions

- What are the three main lessons you can personally take to heart from the Angel Inside?

1.
2.
3.

- What are three actions that you can take today or this month to begin to allow The Angel Inside of you to shine through?

1.
2.
3.

About the Author:

 Chris Widener is an example of how anyone can overcome any odds to achieve a successful life and help others achieve the same. Chris has overcome many obstacles... living through his father dying suddenly when he was four, being sent away from his family to live with relatives at age nine and becoming involved with drugs and alcohol by the age of twelve.

Chris overcame those obstacles and has been speaking professionally since 1988 and has shared the stage with US Presidential candidates, nationally known television news anchors, best-selling authors and professional athletes. He has spoken on motivation and leadership to some of America's finest organizations such as General Electric, Cisco Systems and the Harvard Business School.

Chris has written 350 articles and 5 books and has produced close to 30 audio programs on leadership and motivation. His articles appear monthly in close to 100 publications.

Chris is also a contributor to The Jim Rohn One-Year Success Plan.

The Chris Widener Weekly E-zine, has subscribers in 105 countries, making it one of the world's most widely distributed newsletters on success and leadership.

Chris, his wife Lisa, and their four children make their home in a suburb of Seattle, Washington.

What Others are Saying About Chris Widener:

"I have spoken to more than 3,000 audiences and I can tell you that Chris Widener is one of the best speakers in America today. He is extremely motivational, he is funny, he is sharp, he is quick and to the point. If you are thinking about using him for any reason you can not go wrong with Chris." -- **Brian Tracy, Author "Maximum Achievement**

"A home run every time." -- **Kevin Mather, CFO Seattle Mariners Baseball Team**

"One of the great young speakers that just blew me away is Chris Widener. Chris has the talent, the articulation, the message, the presence, the ability not only as a master of ceremonies, but also as a dynamic presenter. Chris Widener is one of the brand new top stars on the International platform speaking circuit." -- **Denis Waitley, Author "Seeds of Greatness"**

"Challenging and enriching." -- **John Lunde, Student Leader Harvard Business School**

"This guy is nothing short of phenomenal. His patience, his knowledge, his ability to engage with everyone. Chris, you are doing a fabulous job." -- **Jim Rohn, Author "Five Major Pieces to the Life Puzzle"**

"Thought provoking... stirred our imagination." -- **Scott Stull, VP of Sales UniPro, Inc.**

Book Chris Widener to speak at your next event!

Want a speaker who will educate/train your group while instilling humor, excitement and passion? Here are just a few of the topics on which Chris Widener can speak to your business or organization:

- *Leadership Rules of Engagement: Creating Fully Engaged Followers*
- *Leading Your Organization Through Change*
- *The Top Character Traits and Skills of Extraordinary Leaders*
- *Secrets of Motivating Others to Follow Your Leadership*
- *Right Now Leadership: What You Can Do Today to Become a Better Leader*
- *Live the Life You Have Always Dreamed Of!*
- *Dare to Dream*
- *And More!*

Chris is a prolific speaker and writer. He demonstrates a style that is engaging and versatile while providing life-changing principles of leadership, motivation and success.

For more information, contact:

Chris Widener International and/or YourSuccessStore.com
2835 Exchange Boulevard, Suite 200
Southlake, TX 76092
877-929-0439
817-481-9260 DFW Metro
817-442-1390
www.ChrisWidener.com   info@chriswidener.com

Also be sure to sign up for Chris Widener's FREE weekly E-zine!

To Order Additional Copies of Chris Widener's The Angel Inside...

Quantity pricing for *The Angel Inside* (hardback)
(Retail $17.95)

1-9	$12.00 ea
10-24	$9.00 ea
25-99	$6.50 ea
100+	$4.50 ea

Angel
Inside
Photo

Quantity pricing for *The Angel Inside* (paperback)
(Retail $12.95)

1-9	$9.00 ea
10-24	$7.00 ea
25-99	$4.50 ea
100+	$3.00 ea

To order please contact us via any of the following avenues:
1) Call 877-929-0439
2) Email: info@chriswidener.com
3) Visit us on the Web: www.ChrisWidener.com
4) Via mail: Chris Widener International
                 2835 Exchange Blvd., Suite 200
                 Southlake, TX 76092

Look for Chris' New Releases:

Chris Widener and Jim Rohn's new release *The Twelve Pillars*, a fictional story - Michael Jones' car broke down on the side of the road, and when he walked to the nearest house, Michael stumbles across a plantation style mansion on an estate named "Twelve Pillars." Charlie, the maintenance man, helps Michael get back on the road again and also strikes up a relationship with him--and along the way teaches Michael the secrets of success--the Twelve Pillars of Success--that have made the owner of the house, Mr. Davis, a wealthy and successful man.

Secrets of Influence - 12 Characteristics of Dynamic Leaders, Sales People and Top Performers. Based on the Keynote address that Chris gives to organizations all over America, produced solely to help you learn what the successful already know – how to earn wealth, power, recognition and influence that will change your life forever and allow you to live the life of your dreams!

Inspirational Gift Giving Ideas from Jim Rohn,
Denis Waitley, Zig Ziglar and Brian Tracy...

EXCERPTS FROM
THE TREASURY OF QUOTES

These booklets from Denis Waitley, Zig Ziglar,
Brian Tracy & Jim Rohn contain a special **TO...**
and **FROM...** section.

Makes a great gift or addition to any thank you
or holiday card. Perfect for customers,
family and friends!

MIX AND MATCH
PRICING—
SEE BACK PAGE
TO ORDER

Call 877-929-0439
Visit us at YourSuccessStore.com
(Sign up for FREE E-zine)

THE SEEDS OF GREATNESS TREASURY
BY DENIS WAITLEY

The Seeds of Greatness Treasury is a
collection of some of the best-loved words
to remember by "the poet laureat" of
modern-day philosophers, Denis Waitley.
Retail $15.95 each   **Special $12 each**

Let Chris Widener and Jim Rohn help guide you on your journey to personal success…

The Jim Rohn One-Year Success Plan:
A Plan of Consistent and Continual Growth!

We have had 99% of our enrollees stay committed to a plan of consistent and continual growth in their personal and professional lives. The statistics and unsolicited testimonials are astonishing! Simply stated, in 39 plus years, we have never witnessed or been able to match the success and opportunity that The Jim Rohn One-Year Success Plan has generated.

1. A One-Year Game Plan Covering 12 Pillars of Success (one per month - see below) and Geared to Help You Achieve a 10%-40% Increase in the Following:

Month 1)   Personal Development - Become the person you truly desire to be

Month 2)   Goal-setting - multiply your long-term success quotient/clearly defined 10-year goals

Month 3)   Health - Spiritual/Physical/Emotional - Improve your looks, confidence, energy and quality and length of life

Month 4)   Financial Independence/Getting Out of Debt/Saving/Giving

Month 5)   Relationships - Become a more effective and loving parent, spouse and friend

Month 6)   Time Management - Gain between 10 and 15 additional forty-hour work weeks per year

Month 7)   Networking/Referrals - Create more positive influence in the marketplace

Month 8)   Selling/Negotiating - Increase your production by 10%-50%

Month 9)   Communication/Presentation - Increase every level of performance related to your company, staff and personal relationships

Month 10) Leadership - Multiply your efforts and have a positive influence over a larger sphere of people

Month 11) Accelerated Learning - Quickly improve your skills and aptitude to gain and retain knowledge

Month 12) Legacy/Contribution - Take the time to apply your skills in making a difference in your community and world

2. 52 Unique, Weekly Strategic Game Plans via Email with downloadable workbook pages.

3. Receive 12 Conference Calls (one per month) with a specific focus and hosted by a Premier Expert in each of the 12 Pillars of Success including Jim Rohn, Brian Tracy, Zig Ziglar, Patricia Fripp, Bob Burg, Chris Widener and more...

4. Additional Downloadable Books, Audios, Conference Calls and Weekly Workbook Files.

The Silver Package also includes:

5. The Jim Rohn Weekend Event - Excelling in the New Millennium on 20 CDs - includes Jim Rohn, Zig Ziglar, Jeffrey Gitomer, Bob Burg (7 speakers total), Jim's complete 2 day program and 8 bonus sessions/3 days total.

The Gold Package includes:

All benefits listed in Silver Package above PLUS:

6. 21 Hours of DVDs from the Jim Rohn Weekend Event - Excelling in the New Millennium - includes Jim Rohn, Zig Ziglar, Jeffrey Gitomer (7 speakers total), Jim's complete 2-day program and 8 bonus sessions/3 days total.

7. Brian Tracy's Success Mastery Academy - 16 Modules on 16 CDs/Comprehensive Workbook

8. The Jim Rohn Leather Journal

9. Special Bonus - mini seminar conference call each quarter with an expert in a specialized field (Finance, Marketing, Leadership, etc.)

For details go to http://jr1.jimrohn.com or call 800-929-0434.